# Praise for *Sabbath: A Gift of Time*

Bonnie Saul Wilks has blessed us with her articulate description of the place of the Sabbath and provided simple guidelines for observing it in a way that will inspire all of us. It is easy reading, but profound in its clarity. It is especially to be recommended for those who would like a New Covenant way of observing the Sabbath without getting into joy-robbing legalism.

—DON FINTO
Founder of Caleb Company and author of
*Your People Shall Be My People*

What a delightful introduction to the *Shabbat* this booklet provides for those unfamiliar with the history, traditions, and practice of *Shabbat* observance in the home. It even includes interesting recipes for *Shabbat* dinner and the traditional bread "challah," which is served only on the Sabbath. Your understanding of the importance of *Shabbat* as the day of rest will be enriched and strengthened by reading this book.

—RABBI MARTY WALDMAN
Baruch HaShem Congregation, Dallas, Texas

# SABBATH

## A GIFT OF TIME

ETERNAL PROMISE SERIES

# SABBATH
## A GIFT OF TIME

BONNIE SAUL WILKS

*Sabbath: A Gift of Time*
Copyright ©2009, 2018 by Bonnie Saul Wilks
Revised edition
Part of the Eternal Promise series

ISBN: 978-1-945529-52-8 Paperback
ISBN: 978-1-945529-53-5 eBook

We hope you hear from the Holy Spirit and receive God's richest blessings
from this book by Gateway Press. We want to provide the highest quality
resources that take the messages, music, and media of Gateway Church
to the world. For more information on other resources from Gateway
Publishing, go to gatewaypublishing.com.

Gateway Press, an imprint of Gateway Publishing
700 Blessed Way
Southlake, Texas 76092
gatewaypublishing.com

18 19 20 21 22 — 5 4 3 2 1
Printed in the United States of America

Thank you David and Emma Rudolph, founders of Gateways Beyond International in Cyprus, Geneva, Germany, USA, and Israel, and their Messianic missional communities for demonstrating faithfully how to keep, with gladness of heart and fullness of joy, Sabbath principles and celebrations (www.gatewaysbeyond.org).

*What would be a world without Sabbath? It would be a world that knew only itself or God distorted as a thing or the abyss separating Him from the world; a world without the vision of a window in eternity that opens into time.*

—*Abraham Joshua Heschel*

# Table of Contents

# Foreword

AS A JEWISH believer in Jesus, my ministry is dedicated to reaching my people with the Good News of Jesus their Messiah and engaging the Church concerning Israel and the Jewish people. I believe two of the most important verses in the New Testament are found in Romans 11:

> I say then, they did not stumble so as to fall, did they? May it never be! But by their false step salvation has come to the Gentiles, to provoke Israel to jealousy (Romans 11:11 TLV).
>
> For I do not want you, brothers and sisters, to be ignorant of this mystery—lest you be wise in your own eyes—that a partial hardening has come upon Israel until the fullness of the Gentiles has come in; and in this way all Israel will be saved (Romans 11:25–26 TLV).

From the first verse, we learn that every follower of Jesus has a responsibility to provoke the Jewish friend, co-worker, or neighbor in their life to spiritual jealousy. This can only happen when they see in you a depth of faith, love for God, and clarity of purpose they desire to have. They must also come to understand the Messiah you love and serve is the one promised to them in their own Hebrew Scriptures.

The challenge is an almost 2,000-year history of division and animosity between Church and Synagogue, which has resulted in two separate religious institutions with distinct observances and holidays. When a Jewish person hears "Jesus Christ," they immediately think of the "God of Christianity," not the Jewish Messiah, Yeshua. Likewise, most Christians have little understanding or proper appreciation of the connection between their Christian faith and the people and biblical heritage of Israel.

The second verse links the salvation of the Jewish people to the "fullness" of the Gentile Church coming in. Most have understood this to mean the "full number," but I believe this verse refers to something different. Fullness speaks of time, power, authority, and identity. In other words, at the appointed time (the Last Days) when the Church comes back into a fullness of her God-ordained power, authority, and understanding of her identity, it will cause the blindness to lift off the eyes of the Jewish people. An important part of this "fullness of identity" is a re-connection to the Jewish roots of our faith and a clear proclamation to the Jewish people of who Jesus really was and is.

This restoration includes understanding and experiencing the *moed'im* (appointed times) entrusted to the people of Israel. It begins with Shabbat and includes the cycle of observances found in Leviticus 23. These observances are now part of your heritage as a spiritual son or daughter of Abraham. In them, you will find rich, new revelation and a deepening of your relationship with the Lord.

My beloved friend and co-worker, Bonnie Saul Wilks, and her husband, Wayne, have dedicated the last 20-plus years of their lives to working in Jewish ministry with the hope of one day seeing "all Israel saved." I am so grateful for their tireless work and sacrifice. They are living out the mandate of Romans 11:11 and want to help you fulfill your call to do the same.

May this practical guide help you discover and experience the true meaning of Shabbat and introduce you to an exciting new adventure of revelation as you discover the Jewish roots of your faith.

*Rabbi Jonathan Bernis*
President and CEO
Jewish Voice Ministries, International
Phoenix, Arizona

# Preface

I AM HONORED to add small contributions to *Sabbath: A Gift of Time*, which my wife originally wrote and published in 2009.

Bonnie has especially carried the burden to encourage believers in Jesus on the beautiful lessons they can learn from the Friday evening Sabbath meal, and practicing weekly rest.

We encourage you to read this book as if you were receiving "a gift of time," and not from a legal perspective, or something you "must do." Rather, I pray you will be encouraged in the eternal principles of rest, worship, and family.

We are living in the days when some are growing more interested in liturgy. While this book does not intend to provide a definitive "form" for celebrating the Sabbath, we do pray it will be a path to guide you.

May God use this book to provide basic knowledge of Sabbath tradition, which you can adapt to create a life-giving experience for you and your family.

*Wayne Wilks, Jr, PhD*
Executive Pastor Jewish Ministries at
Gateway Church and President Emeritus, MJBI

# Acknowledgments

OUR DAUGHTER, JULIA, who loves the family gathering of Sabbath.

Our parents, Benjamin and Marjorie Saul, and Wayne and Carol Wilks, who instilled in us a love for the Jewish people and the Church.

Olen and Syble Griffing, who have been spiritual parents to us, launched us into Jewish ministry, and have loved us unconditionally for over 30 years.

Our pastors, Robert and Debbie Morris, who have faithfully heralded the historic, present, and prophetic place of the Jewish people, and allowed us to serve Gateway Church.

Valentin and Tatyana Sviontek, who pioneered the first Messianic Jewish Bible Institute with us in Odessa, Ukraine, and celebrated many Sabbaths with us around the world.

Yura and Katya Mokhort, special friends in Russia, and all the directors and staff of the Messianic Jewish Bible Institutes abroad who are on the frontlines serving the Jewish people.

Laurinda Dunn, who untangled our first efforts at scribbling, piecing it together like a jigsaw puzzle that finally made sense.

Jonathan Bernis and the MJBI board, who opened many doors of opportunity in Jewish ministry around the world.

Dr. Daniel C. Juster, who offered help with theological content.

Nic Lesmeister, Alisa Stephenson, Carol Adams, Yuan Wang, and the staff of the MJBI USA administrative office, who have worked tirelessly in serving the mission and vision of MJBI around the world.

Our Publishers at Gateway Publishing, Craig Dunnagan, John Andersen, Kathy Krenzien, Jenny Morgan, Peyton Sepeda, James Reid, and Caleb Jobe, who saw the potential in this book to further the mission of Gateway Church—"to the Jew first."

# Sabbath Foundations

*Israel is given Sabbath as a memorial of God's
gracious rescue from slavery as well as a
memorial of creation, and God's resting
in the seventh period.*

—*Daniel Juster*

MORE SACRED THAN the Day of Atonement, the Sabbath
celebration eclipses all Jewish holy days and feasts. It is a day of
exceptional beauty and holiness. Mystics, rabbis, and observers
through the ages have written about its ethereal quality, its
wonder, its reward, and its miracle.

My first *Erev Shabbat* (Sabbath Evening) experience
occurred in Israel when I was in my early 20s. That evening
was like a shaft of light piercing through a dark cloud with a
beauty that captivated my heart.

As we walked into Kibbutz Einat's dining room[1] with the
local Israelis, candles flickered on tables covered with white
cloths. Many of the women wore simple skirts and blouses, and

---

[1] A *kibbutz* is a communal farm in Israel, which began in the late 1800s for the
purpose of building up the wasteland of what was then called Palestine. Today
there are over 300 *kibbutzim* (Hebrew plural) in Israel. The *kibbutz* style of
community has been very successful in Israel, spanning nearly four generations
since its inception. Kibbutz Einat is located near Petach Tikvah, Israel.

the men were dressed in jeans and white shirts, in contrast to their everyday, casual style. The atmosphere rang of celebration, and the aroma of baked chicken and onion gravy filled the dining room.

As a non-Jew, I experienced a deep sense of belonging and longing at the same time. I had stumbled upon a missing puzzle piece in life, the order of which began to answer unexplained questions that had nagged me about the life-in-the-fast-lane pace which had enslaved me.

On that Sabbath twilight—just one special evening in an ordinary week—all of the circumstances of my life paled compared to the soothing refuge of time that this experience offered. My body let go of its strain. My soul let go of its worry. My heart let go of its care and settled into peace; the kind of tranquility that God promises to those who eat of the fruit of weekly rest.

I relished the sense of peace that I felt during that delightful evening meal; it was as if God had given me a sanctuary, a clear break from the workaday world. The Sabbath carried me through the quiet calm of a relaxing next day and prepared me for the upcoming week. And in a real way, it equipped me for my life's calling.

Since that time, my family has enjoyed many such days of Sabbath peace and respite. Some experiences took place in crude and unrefined places, while others have been in luxury and opulence. I have vivid memories of cold *Erev Shabbat* meals in Odessa, Ukraine, where our teeth chattered as we lifted our glasses to bless the God of Israel. Our hearts flooded with joy as we ushered in the hallowed evening in an austere Ukrainian home with no heat and little food, and we sensed God's eternal purpose. Once we observed the Sabbath in a six-star hotel in Addis Ababa, Ethiopia, which was in stark contrast to the abject poverty on the streets outside. We have celebrated in countries like Argentina, Ethiopia, Zimbabwe, Brazil, Cyprus, Hungary, Russia, Israel, and the United States; with Jews, Christians, Catholics, Orthodox, and Messianic Jews[2] alike. And in each place, no matter the physical surroundings, a spirit of love, brotherhood, family, and harmony have greeted us. Those early impressions of keeping the Sabbath have never left me, and continue to enrich my life as I strive to follow hard after God by setting aside a day especially for Him.

When we first began to keep the Sabbath in earnest, it was a battle. Life's demands drove us hard and fast, and there was no time to slow down, much less pause and rejuvenate. At first, we swallowed Sabbath observance like medicine; like a *bitter* pill that was *good* for us. The bitter was the discipline it took to make ourselves rest. The good was the tremendous benefit of "letting down" for a complete day. It became a joy to stop and rest—to do what we wanted or even what we didn't want.

We did not approach Sabbath-keeping legalistically by minutes, or hours, or by a definition of work. Our guidelines sprang from within—I believe from the Holy Spirit, who gave us a "sense" of what was either replenishing or draining us. That is the "law" of *Shabbat* break to which we adhere, even to this day.

We have found great liberation in such discipline. Because we travel extensively as a couple, we may not prepare a Sabbath

---

[2] A Messianic Jew is a Jew who has come to faith in Jesus, *Yeshua* in Hebrew, as the Messiah of Israel, Son of God, and Savior of the world. They do not believe that when a Jew comes to faith in Jesus that he/she ceases to be Jewish and becomes Christian. They claim the same place in the Church that the first generation of Jewish believers in Jesus enjoyed, and they are in no way compromised as God's chosen people.

meal and enjoy the Sabbath liturgy every week; however, we do take time to rest wherever we are. We have discovered that resting and recreating routinely bring harmony and order to life—something we desperately need to be productive the other six days of the week.

The benefits far outweigh the inconveniences. Now we are almost "addicted" to Sabbath rest and understand why God placed it in the Commandments. The frail human form must stop to recreate in order to live a healthy life ... to continue creating and producing ... as our Creator designed us to do.

The offering of Sabbath peace that comes from the one true God of Abraham, Isaac, and Jacob still draws Jewish people and Christians today, from all nations. There is a renewed desire to learn the Sabbath's ancient remedies. Many are discovering its restorative power and applying it to their hectic lifestyles, just as we have.

This book is a glimpse into the miracle God called *Shabbat*, and it stands as a testimony that God demonstrated the value of *Shabbat* thousands of years ago. He continues to offer dry and weary souls a refreshing fountain, for those who will take the time to drink of Sabbath rest.

# CHAPTER 1

# Three Purposes

THE OBSERVANCE OF the Sabbath serves many purposes. Both the Bible and Jewish Sabbath prayer books outline three expectations.

1.  A ceremonial celebration remembering the Israelites' redemption from Egyptian slavery (Exodus 13:1–16).
2.  A ceremonial celebration honoring God's creation of the universe in six days, and His resting or ceasing from work on the seventh (Genesis 2:1–3).
3.  A glimpse and foretaste of the "Age to Come"—what it will be like in Messianic times (Ezekiel 36:16–38).

These three purposes serve as the foundation of Sabbath practice, although the second reason rises above the other two. Rest is critical to humanity's well-being. Locked within the three-letter Hebrew root for Sabbath is a key to understanding God's intention for this day: It means to halt or to cease. We cannot rest without coming to a full stop. Slowing down doesn't do the job of physical, mental, and emotional restoration. Ceasing activity prepares the body and the soul for replenishing rest. With the routine practice of keeping the Sabbath, the other two purposes start to become clearer and we can see more of the beauty of this discipline.

# CHAPTER 2

# A Blessing and Not a Burden

ACCORDING TO LEGEND, rabbis wondered what God meant when He said in Genesis that on the seventh day He finished the work that He had been doing (Genesis 2:2). The rabbis reasoned that God had created the world in six days, but what was still missing? The only thing creation lacked was rest—peace and quiet. God added Sabbath, the day of respite, to make the week complete and perfect, they concluded.

The foundation and meaning of Sabbath runs deeper than it first appears. Its observance goes beyond God's need for rest, peace, and quiet after the six days of creation. After all, God wasn't "tired" after his creation labors. I believe the Lord of all creation sat back to enjoy what He spoke into existence, just as any master builder would.

As a stained glass artist, I enjoy and savor my completed pieces, often returning to view them after my hours of labor. I like to soak in their beauty and artistry, and to explore their flaws or discover how to improve my next piece. Sometimes, I call my husband and daughter in to view what I have created. I think that is one of the most important reasons God stopped to rest; He paused to absorb it all. His vast creation was so magnificent, so exquisite, so beyond human understanding—truly worthy of a day of honor. The Designer invites us to stop, along with Him, to enjoy life by resting and recreating ourselves. It is a small request compared to the gift of life and the beauty around us.

King Solomon wrote, "It is the glory of God to conceal a matter and the glory of kings to search it out" (Proverbs 25:2 TLV). The true benefits of the Sabbath lie concealed beneath the surface; we must strip away our other feeble attempts to "rest" by "resting" on the seventh day. The Lord knows that we may try and then fail many times. Eventually, however, we begin to enrich our bodies, souls, and spirits. We uncover physical and spiritual riches, which He has left for the taking.

Sabbath-keeping laws are many and detailed. The *Mishnah*[1] describes them as "mountains hanging by a hair," for "there is little Scripture and many rules." Because the Bible gives few concrete instructions on how to keep the Sabbath, the rabbis developed detailed guidelines about the holiest day of the week. The purpose of this book is to simplify and demystify the observance of the Sabbath.

Those who set aside a day from work experience a marvelous blessing—a sense of tranquility and sacredness. The Sabbath is clearly a gift from a wise and loving God who knows that we must cease from work to replenish on a regular basis. He wants to bless us with a wonderful treasure—a gift of time.

[1] The first section of the Talmud, a collection of early oral interpretations of the Scriptures compiled about AD 200.

# CHAPTER 3

# Not Just for Israel

ALTHOUGH GOD GAVE Sabbath as a commandment to Israel, it extended to other nations and cultures. Centuries ago, those who remembered and observed the Sabbath greatly influenced the general population of Rome, although ancient authors spoke of it with distaste, even contempt and ridicule. They called it a "superstitious practice of laziness." But the Roman Jewish historian, Josephus, described the spread of Sabbath practices throughout the Roman Empire, including the lighting of Sabbath candles. Perhaps this observance continued because Roman Jews throughout the empire, who came to faith in Jesus, maintained their Jewish identity and practices. The first followers of Jesus were Jewish and maintained their Jewish lifestyles. It is not difficult to visualize the first Messianic Jews warmly and ceremoniously observing this special day, particularly in light of the events that had taken place after the death and resurrection of Jesus.

Later, Christians incorporated Sabbath-keeping into their theology, but they changed the day to Sunday because it commemorated the resurrection of Jesus. Muslims also observe a day of rest and assembly on Friday, in which they permit work, but also hold prayer services.

# CHAPTER 4

# A Source of Jewish Longevity

HAS SABBATH-KEEPING HAD anything to do with how long the Jews have lasted as a people? God's ancient people have existed for 3,500 years, longer than any other people group. Early American author Mark Twain marveled at this fact and asked himself the same question. His thoughts in *Concerning the Jews* are intriguing. He wrote:

> If the statistics are right, the Jews constitute but one percent of the human race. It suggests a nebulous dim puff of star dust lost in the blaze of the Milky Way. Properly, the Jew ought hardly to be heard of, but he is heard of, has always been heard of. He is as prominent on the planet as any other people ... His contributions to the world's list of great names in literature, science, art, music, finance, medicine, and abstruse learning are also way out of proportion to the weakness of his numbers. He has made a marvelous fight in the world, in all the ages; and has done it with his hands tied behind him.
>
> The Egyptian, the Babylonian, and the Persian rose, filled the planet with sound and splendor, then faded to dream-stuff and passed away; the Greek and the Roman followed, and made a vast noise, and they are gone; other peoples have sprung up and held their torch high for a time, but it burned out, and they sit in twilight now, or have vanished ....

All things are mortal but the Jew; all other forces pass, but he remains. What is the secret of his immortality?[1]

Many reasons exist for the prolonged survival of the Jewish people. Two of them stand out from all others: their ritual observance of the Sabbath and the Jewish festivals, and the covenant-keeping power of a mighty and loving God. When considering what has kept the Jewish nation together for thousands of years, we must understand what it means to honor a special day each week.

Sabbath is at the heart of Judaism. Its observance crystallizes the meaning of the Jewish calling. From it flow all Jewish traditions, biblical or rabbinical. Rabbis advised wandering Jews that wished to return to their foundation of faith to begin keeping the Sabbath in earnest. When Sabbath is in place, other Jewish traditions, feasts, and practices also fall into place naturally.

Sabbath is considered the holiest of all the Jewish holidays and is perhaps the most misunderstood by both Jews and Gentiles. Therefore, it is essential for Christians and Messianic Jews to take a deeper look at the observance of Sabbath to unlock its treasures and to apply them to their modern lifestyles. Somehow, through the ages, those who have set aside a day for restoration of the body, soul, and spirit have tapped into a fountain of strength and endurance that has lasted for at least 3,500 years.

One of the most common complaints I hear from neighbors, friends, co-workers, and family is "There just isn't enough time." Everyone suffers from the trade-off of time versus obligation. We all have similar responsibilities to earn a living, nurture a family, care for parents, invest quality time in

---

[1] Mark Twain, "Concerning The Jews," *Harper's Magazine*, March 1898.

children, cook, exercise, clean house, squeeze in entertainment and vacation, develop hobbies and friendships, and so forth ... there are just not enough hours in the day to do it all.

It may surprise you that to find time, you must sacrifice or spend it in new ways. New Testament teaching consists of many of Jesus' ironic ideas: to find life you must die; to receive you must give; and to bless those who curse you. Jesus said these choices would usher in the kingdom of God. That is His principality of light reigning in a dark and fallen world. I like to call it His kingdom of opposites.

As believers, we know this kingdom of opposites is real and effective. We cannot see it fully with our eyes, but we feel it, live in it, and know it is real. Jesus dared His followers to live an ironic life by commanding them to "love those who hate you," or respond to life in an abnormal, almost super-human way. It's hard, but we know it works. We also know it is impossible without the Holy Spirit.

The Lord based His plea to stop and rest on irony as well. We can accomplish *more* by *doing* less. This kind of ironic living develops faith—as we make decisions to do things that seem unusual or out of the normal. Observant Jews have tapped into this principle for centuries, and it is the source of their staying power. They have learned to unwrap the gift of time through the sacrifice of time.

We find another clue regarding Jewish longevity in one of the Sabbath songs: *Am Yisrael chai. Ode avenue chai,* which means: "The people of Israel live. The forefathers of Israel still live." Jewish people and their ancestors continued to keep their traditions over the centuries. The remembrance and observance of Sabbath and the Jewish feasts produce fruit that links the generations.

These strong cords of survival have knitted the Jewish people together through a harrowing history of dispersion, near extermination, and relentless wandering. God, in the first five books of the Bible—the *Torah*—detailed laws that have protected them to this day. It was not the wisdom of the laws themselves that kept watch over the Jews, but rather their observance and remembrance of these statutes that have helped them outlive all other ethnic groups.

God is not like a man who lies; He clearly states through the prophet Jeremiah that His covenant with the Jewish people will last as long as the heavens and the foundations of the world (Jeremiah 31:37). When considering God's ancient people, we cannot overestimate the longsuffering kindness of an almighty God, who faithfully keeps the promises He has made to them. God linked His eternal arms with His covenant nation and as they returned their grip, through ritual and law, it has protected their distinctiveness and ensured their longevity as a nation among nations.

# CHAPTER 5

# Sabbath Restores

ORIGINALLY, I APPROACHED the subject of Sabbath-keeping as a casual observer. My deep love and respect first sprang up in my heart for the special day of rest while living on a *kibbutz* while I was in my early twenties. However, only in the last twenty years has my family become serious partakers in the restorative power that comes with honoring this holy day.

We discovered that we couldn't fully realize the benefits of Sabbath by only keeping one or two days a year. To achieve the full benefit of Sabbath requires habitual remembrance and observance. It is a discipline, and its reward grows through faithful practice. The true effects of any exercise come from constant practice rather than sporadic effort, and so it is with the honoring of the Sabbath day.

Life tempts me to press on with activities that never quit nipping at my heels, but the appeal of that "busyness" grows dimmer. I will never forget standing in a long line at a grocery store on a Saturday morning, trying to "get a little extra accomplished" before we flew out on an extended international trip the next day. I was exhausted and angry by the time I returned home, and the whole experience dampened the joy of preparing to travel. I should have kept my feet up on the back porch, sipping ice tea. I could have gotten up early the next day to do the extra shopping.

# CHAPTER 6

# As Old as Creation

MOST PEOPLE DON'T remember that Sabbath respite sprang out of creation. Instead, they think of the Ten Commandments as the original law outlining the importance of keeping the Sabbath holy. However, God declared a day of rest after His six days of creating (Genesis 2:1–3). He blessed the seventh day and sanctified it (or set it apart) from all other days. Our finite minds can barely grasp that the infinite Creator took a day of rest.

If God, the Supreme Being of the universe, took time to rest and reflect at the end of a six-day work period, then how much more should we frail humans follow His example? God's example also implies that this pause from work is good for all humanity, not just the Jewish people. Adam and Eve weren't Jewish. God created them many years before Abraham, the father of Judaism. God intended Sabbath-keeping to be a gift for all of His creation.

God's example shows just how serious He was *and is* in revealing to us our need for a weekly break. God instructed the Israelites after they left Egypt to gather extra manna on the sixth day (Exodus 16:5). God told them not to collect on the seventh day, but rather to rest. The Jewish people who came out from Egypt with Moses experienced many *Shabbats* together. It probably didn't take them long to learn the importance and reward of rest. If they tried to gather manna on the Sabbath, they found nothing. They discovered their efforts were useless, and they went hungry! God forced them to rest by withholding nourishment and not rewarding their attempts to work. Their growling stomachs reminded them to gather enough food on the sixth day in preparation for the seventh day's rest.

# CHAPTER 7

# A Universal Need

YOU MIGHT FIND it difficult to appreciate the Orthodox Jewish observances of Sabbath laws that forbid work. Those laws stand in stark contrast to the principles of accumulating wealth, increasing knowledge, or pursuing pleasure. These principles dominate many cultures, especially in the West. That level of effort seems to make sense in materialistic societies. Many believe that seven days of work will produce greater gain and contentment than six days will. This erroneous thought process makes it easy to forego one of God's most precious gifts to humanity: an appointed time to rest.

Our need for rest, however, is universal. Over the centuries, Gentiles who also love the God of Abraham, Isaac, and Jacob have debated whether they should engage in Sabbath practice. Others claim the Church is in error because it does not keep the Sabbath. Contemporary Messianic Jewish author, scholar, and theologian, Daniel Juster wrote in his article "Is the Church Pagan?"

> The claim is also made that Christians are pagan because they do not keep the commandments of God. They do not keep the Sabbath on the Seventh Day, the major Feasts of the Bible, and the food laws. I recognize that the Sabbath will be universal in the Age to Come. The Age to Come may include the

universalization of the major feasts. However, the Bible explicitly
names only the Sabbath and Tabernacles as universal. My view
is that the apostolic decision in Acts 15 loosed Gentiles from
responsibility for these commandments (Acts 15, Galatians 5).
Yes, they can be celebrated by all. Yes, they should be a context
for much of our understanding of *Yeshua*. Yes, Messianic Jewish
congregations should be respected for keeping them. Yet there is
not one word in the New Testament that makes these a covenant
responsibility for the Church as a whole.[1]

Juster believes that the principles of Sabbath observance
may be a guide for all, although Christians remain free to
integrate these practices on Sundays or on another day.
Believers should look to Jesus who declared that He was the
Lord of the Sabbath (Mark 2:28). His example will help them
derive practical understanding and application on how to
observe the seventh day of rest.[2]

The true spirit of keeping Sabbath, which focuses on restoration of the body, soul, and spirit and not the burden of the
law, empowers and invigorates the weariest soul. Even the
casual observer of Jewish life will unlock curative treasures
in its keeping. To maintain the Sabbath rabbinical law strictly
forbids thirty-nine acts of labor, such as transporting, baking,
harvesting, lighting a fire, plowing, cleaning, and most of all
creating. For those who adhere to these restrictions, it is a step
of faith to cease all productivity of material life for twenty-four
hours to concentrate on refreshing spiritual life.

---

[1] Daniel Juster, "Is the Church Pagan?" *Israel's Restoration* 13, no.3 (March
2004).
[2] Daniel Juster, *Jewish Roots,* (Rockville, Maryland: DAVAR Publishing, 1986),
195.

# CHAPTER 8

# Suggestion or Commandment?

JEWS WHO KEEP the Sabbath will set timers for appliances and lights or unscrew refrigerator bulbs before sundown on Friday evenings to avoid the slightest hint of labor. Although this example may seem strict, there is profound beauty hidden within Sabbath ceremony that is worth unlocking. Sabbath formalities promise a far broader and deeper reward than mere adherence to regulations might initially suggest.

Many Jews and non-Jews regard the keeping of Sabbath as a suggestion, although it stands as the fourth of the Ten Commandments that God gave Moses on Mount Sinai; one which carried the death penalty if it was broken. Its significant instruction is nestled among principles that have become the framework of societies for centuries: do not murder, do not steal, do not commit adultery, and honor your parents. Rabbi Lawrence A. Hoffman writes that most people's attitude toward observing the Sabbath and keeping it holy is that it is optional:

"Here are nine commandments—and a suggestion."[1]

God has designed Sabbath faithfulness as far more than a suggestion. Some scholars and theologians have said the

[1] Rachel S. Mikva, ed., *Broken Tablets—Restoring the Ten Commandments and Ourselves* (Woodstock, VT: Jewish Lights Publishing, 1999).

Sabbath is what kept Israel alive as a nation. Ancient Israel's surrounding neighbors had no equivalent of Sabbath or *Shabbat*. Early Babylonians remembered a day of rest called *Shappatu* during a full moon once a month, but it was considered a day of bad luck, much like some regard Friday the 13th today. Romans and Greeks had no day of rest like Sabbath and ultimately persecuted Jews for their Sabbath traditions.[2]

---

[2] Amy A. Freedman, *Don't Forget the Sabbath Spice,* *https://amyfreedman.net/2014/12/07/dont-forget-the-sabbath-spice/.*

# CHAPTER 9

# Not Always Convenient

DURING THE MIDDLE AGES, Jewish families throughout Europe and Russia would do without during the week in order to splurge on a festive meal for Friday night. The meal was elaborate with special foods and recipes. Jewish communities sometimes helped those who could not afford a Sabbath meal. But through the years, some have not consistently kept the Sabbath simply because they found it economically or socially inconvenient.

Although greater affluence exists in much of the Jewish world today, some find these restrictions too limiting. Secular Jews choose the observances that most fit their lifestyles, such as only lighting candles or eating a special meal. Individual families vary their practices according to their preferences. Even so, a great resurgence of Sabbath practice is emerging.

A few years ago, I met a European young man who grew up as a Messianic Christian. That is to say, his parents embraced Jewish lifestyle and practice and added it to their already Christian way of life. They celebrated all the feasts, including the Sabbath. Some Gentile Christians read and understand the Bible and want to partake of the commonwealth of Israel in their everyday lives. Some may say this is like trying to mix oil and water, but this phenomenon is occurring over and over as the Church begins to awaken to Israel's significance through the ages, today, and prophetically. God's design is slowly coming together as we see the One New Man (Ephesians 2:14) in rudimentary form as Gentile and Jew unite under the banner of our common Redeemer, *Yeshua,* without offense or barrier.

In Southlake, Texas, Gateway Church loves God's chosen people and dedicates a Messianic Jewish service at the first of each month to Jewish believers. The Messianic pastors teach about biblical truths derived from the study and observance of keeping the Jewish feasts, especially the Sabbath. Gateway Church gives a tenth of the church's tithe to Jewish ministry first each month before the church pays any other expenses. Founding Senior Pastor Robert Morris teaches that the Scripture means exactly what it says, that the gospel is "For the Jew first" (Romans 1:16).

The leaders of Gateway's monthly Messianic Service encourage those who attend to keep the Jewish holidays, not legalistically, but to partake of the riches of God's Word and biblical Jewish tradition. There is so much of *Yeshua* locked within celebration of the feast days that honoring them grows more precious with time. Observance proves they are life-giving and rewarding, not burdensome.

In the past, Jews sometimes risked their wealth and even their lives to keep the Sabbath set apart in holy reverence. In defiance of suppression, domination, and a genocide called the Holocaust, keeping of the Sabbath prevailed as the foundation of Jewish survival. Sabbath remembrance and observance are central to Jewish life, whether or not they are convenient.

# CHAPTER 10

# Approaching Sabbath as Holy Ground

SCRIPTURE SHOWS THAT the Sabbath is the first thing God declared holy. Therefore, great benefit comes from approaching Sabbath as holy ground. Moses stood upon holy ground at the burning bush (Exodus 3:1–10). The Hebrew root word for holy is *kadosh* and means "set apart from the common." That is exactly what holy ground is—an uncommon place of profound meaning set apart from the ordinary.

As Moses tended his sheep, he stumbled upon that burning bush. His curiosity piqued, so he came closer. Moses drew near, and God called him by name, "Moses." In that remote place, at " ... the farthest end of the wilderness ... " (Exodus 3:1 TLV), in the presence of a bush in flames but not consumed, God gave Moses instructions that changed his life, and the history of the Jewish nation, forever. Moses grew humble and covered his face. The God of the universe shared His heart for the hurting Hebrew slaves and revealed His plan of deliverance. It is nothing short of miraculous how God unburdened His heart to Moses.

This Exodus passage shows the intimacy that is possible between God and people when they come together upon holy ground. In those places, the Lord will call your name, you will be humbled, and you will receive life-changing instruction.

Each Sabbath, as you set the day apart from the common workweek to rest, think of wherever you are as holy ground. Allow God to call your name and reveal His heart to you. You will begin to want every day to be Sabbath as you learn to give God time to know you intimately and you receive new revelation. You will begin to equate the gift of time with tender dialogue between you and the infinite Creator of all life. He wants to guide your steps and give you keys to an abundant life. But for that to happen, you must make the sacrifice of time to be alone with the most holy God in a holy place.

# CHAPTER 11

# Centered in the Home

THE JEWISH COMMUNITY has traditionally maintained synagogues for feasts or appointed times of service in the temple, where twelve loaves of bread were present and displayed—which are also known as the Showbread. Each *Shabbat*, these loaves were carefully placed on the table of the sanctuary in two rows of six and sprinkled with frankincense. Later, the priests ate the loaves, and then replaced them for the next *Shabbat* (Leviticus 24:5–9). Some scholars believe those loaves symbolized the twelve tribes of Israel; others think they mirror the presence of God. Messianic Jews consider both possibilities as true, being harmoniously intertwined symbols of God's living-bread presence and ever-abiding covenant with His ancient people.

After the destruction of the second temple and the dispersion of the Jewish nation in AD 70, the synagogue and the Jewish home became the central places to keep *Shabbat*. Since then, rabbinical Sabbath liturgy evolved and became more formalized. No matter how elaborate the synagogue ritual, the Jewish home remains the focal point of remembering *Shabbat* and keeping it holy. With the temple's destruction, Jews were scattered into other countries. They had no designated place to honor the Sabbath. Practice began to center on the home and remains that way, even now.

Consideration of the Sabbath runs throughout the week. Sabbath is a bit like celebrating Thanksgiving each week, and its execution takes much thought and preparation. On Friday morning, Jewish homes across the world buzz with activity: housecleaning, food buying and preparation, and making sure the children are dressed and bathed. Then the hour arrives as though a gift arrived from heaven. Some observers attend synagogues or churches to pray and remember traditions on Friday evening or Saturday. But for the most part, the celebration of Sabbath rest takes place in the warmth of the home.

I sit in Jerusalem as I write this, and the Sabbath draws close. Israeli Jews scurry about the ancient city in preparation. However, in a few hours, this busy life will come to a screeching halt. Silence will reign for 24 hours. The door to rest and rejuvenation will gently open, and for those who are willing, a gift will appear ... time. In Israel, the greeting "Shabbat Shalom" is best understood as *Sabbath peace.* To understand it, you must experience it.

# CHAPTER 12

# The Resurgence of Sabbath

MESSIANIC JEWS AND many others are zealously resurrecting the observance of *Shabbat*, especially in nations whose governments have restricted religious freedoms. Messianic congregations[1] encourage and teach *Shabbat* practice to new Jewish believers. The Messianic Jewish Bible Institute operates in many countries throughout the world.[2] The institute provides instruction in "Messianic Jewish Life and Practice," which is a class that teaches Jewish practices to those who have lost touch

[1] Many Messianic Jews have established congregations throughout the world. Some Jewish believers maintain a Jewish lifestyle while remaining members of nominal churches. Recent statistics estimate there are over 15,000 Messianic Jews in Israel who belong to vibrant Messianic congregations. These communities and places of worship seek to model New Covenant Jewish followers of Jesus in life and practice as illustrated in the Book of Acts. They usually meet on the Sabbath (Saturday) and use Davidic music and dance, and practice Jewish traditions consistent with biblical truth. Although there has always been an expression of this movement, the Holy Spirit has resurrected Messianic congregations in ever-increasing numbers since the 1960s. Congregations stand in agreement with both the Old and New Testaments and Jesus' work to create the One New Man. Membership is open to both Jew and Gentile, and the focus is to be a culturally relevant expression to reach Jewish communities with the Good News of *Yeshua*.

[2] The Messianic Jewish Bible Institute trains young messianic believers, and those called to Jewish ministry, for leadership positions in Messianic congregations. It was pioneered in 1996 in Odessa, Ukraine, and is located in Ethiopia, Zimbabwe, Ukraine, Russia, Argentina, Brazil, Korea, Israel, Hungary, Mexico, and Israel. For more information see www.mjbi.org.

with their traditions. The class teaches them to cherish, rekindle, and observe all Jewish feasts in their homes. The observance of the Sabbath takes top priority.

Today, Christians are eager to learn more about the Sabbath and its keeping. Many believers have begun to awaken to the importance of the biblical Jewish feasts in general. Since Wayne and I are engaged in Jewish ministry and travel frequently in the US and internationally, church leaders as well as ordinary Christians constantly ask us about Jewish and biblical traditions regarding the Sabbath.

The Holy Spirit is at work reinforcing ancient biblical truths, and people are beginning to seek the beauty of Sabbath practice in their homes and churches. Many are simply in need of rest. Celebrating Sabbath while accepting God's gift of time has strengthened and encouraged believers in their faith, as well as improved their well-being.

# CHAPTER 13

# The Father's Role

## Wayne Wilks, Jr, PhD

ONE OF THE foundational and outstanding aspects of Gateway Church is the principle of rest. Through the teaching and example of Founding Senior Pastor Robert Morris, Gateway Church has set a high value on developing the discipline of routinely and weekly taking a break from the demands of work. Pastor Morris' example as a man and a leader in his home and the church speaks to me. He encourages me to take leadership as I teach my family the value of time off. Pastor Morris writes of the Sabbath:

> I quickly learned that as an organization [Gateway Church] we must think and act intentionally about the Sabbath. What we have endeavored—and are still endeavoring—to do is cultivate a culture of rest. Like everything else, I know the establishment of this value begins with me.[1]

Since the family at home takes center stage for Sabbath, the father should gently lead his wife and children to embrace the gift of rest that God the Father has given us. The mother prepares the way for this special weekly event by cleaning,

[1] Robert Morris, *The Blessed Church*, (Colorado Springs: Waterbrook Press, 2012), 184.

cooking, preparing the children, making the evening and day special. Meanwhile, the father sets the example for keeping and observing the day in word and deed.

The father's presence and actions speak louder than any words voiced during Sabbath liturgy. He lifts the bread and the cup and blesses the God of heaven who made and gave these life-sustaining elements. The father lays his hands on his children's heads and speaks a blessing and prayer over them every week. Then he draws close to his wife and speaks approval and encouragement on her as well.

Throughout a busy week, words of praise may fall through the cracks. But the father has the opportunity to perform blessings on the Sabbath. He can tune in to each child and speak the traditional blessings that God's people have expressed for centuries. The father may also say things from his heart. Verbal commendation has the power to heal wounds from the past and set the stage for a bright future. The father may even speak prophetic words, leading his children into unknown and unseen, yet righteous pathways. These words of praise let his offspring know that he sees and cares about both the large and small things of their lives.

During the Sabbath evening meal in our home, my daughter Julia looks forward to this time of special words and prayer. My wife does as well. Rarely do I hear men praise their wives openly in social settings. My wife has really become the hero of my life, and this time of special acknowledgement barely allows me to begin giving back to her for the sacrifices she makes for me and our family. These words of affirmation can be healing as well.

Scripture lifts up the importance of male leadership. Though we are frail and human, the Bible's fathers had important roles in the lives of their families. Abraham, father of the Jewish nation, struck out on his own to follow God with nothing but raw faith. His descendants would become as numerous as the stars and the sand. Noah saved the human race. Joseph saved his nation. The Scripture provides so many examples of male leadership. We have a rich treasure chest from which to draw.

When a father displays leadership during the Sabbath evening meal's liturgy, and when he takes steps to rest with his family, those acts help establish his role in the home. According to Scripture, a census in Israel traditionally counted the males:

> "Take a census of the whole Israelite community by their clans and families, listing every man by name, one by one" (Numbers 1:2 NIV).

During those times, the leadership role of the father in the family was significant. His role in Hebrew society was so important that the census was taken according to the number of men. Every culture in the world has had this test—will the males stand and be counted? Many nations have changed these roles for the family, eliminating or diminishing the role of husbands and fathers. Even American culture has, sadly, begun to lean in this direction.

Fathers' leading the way for their families in spiritual disciplines and practices is extremely important for the survival of the family. When fathers lead by example in Sabbath rest and the weekly giving of fatherly and priestly blessings, they show the church and the world that they are laying down their lives for their families.

Of course, in some homes no father figure is present. The mother should then take the leadership role in directing Sabbath rest and offering the blessings over the wine, bread, and family. God gives special grace to women who parent alone. They have a very difficult, yet noble, role.

# CHAPTER 14

# God of Time

ABRAHAM JOSHUA HESCHEL is a Jewish scholar, author, and theologian whose thoughts on time opened my eyes and started a revolution in my heart. He says that time is more important to God than things or places. We understand the God of the Jews better through the abstractness of time than we do through our other senses. Genesis introduces God to the world through the concept of time:

> In the beginning, God created the heavens and the earth (Genesis 1:1 TLV).

All believers know God as the beginning and ending of time:

> I AM the Alpha and the Omega, the First and the Last, the Beginning and the End (Revelation 22:13 TLV).

According to Heschel, we see the main themes of Jewish faith in the concept of time rather than place: the new moon, the festivals, the jubilee year, and the Sabbath. All of these depend upon a certain day and season. In Jewish life, designated times during the year usher in a call for prayer, celebration, or fasting. Jews remember the Day of Atonement, the Jewish New Year, the Feast of Tabernacles, and the Passover. Jews have long understood God through the calendar. One of God's greatest gifts is the gift of time found in observance of *Shabbat*.

Blessings result when we honor the *Shabbat*. Curses happen when people neglect it. That holy time, specified by God, is important. Heschel writes:

> The mystical mind would expect that, after heaven and earth have been established, God would create a holy place—a holy mountain or a holy spring—whereupon a sanctuary is to be established. Yet it seems as if to the Bible it is holiness in time, the Sabbath, which comes first.[1]

*Kadosh*, the Hebrew word for holy, is a powerful word in the Bible. It emphasizes the mystery and magnificence of God and is a window into His character. Heschel says, "The first thing that God called *kadosh* was the seventh day." God demonstrated its significance when He expressed the Jewish concept of holiness in terms of time rather than materialism.[2]

Time has become the enemy of people. We cannot control it. It puts pressure on us daily as we age. It changes things irrevocably, and it indulges no one. Contemporary society trades time for gaining more things and seeking more pleasure.

Heschel calls *Shabbat* a palace in time. He writes that the Sabbaths are our great cathedrals.[3] His metaphor evokes memories of some of the historic synagogues and cathedrals scattered throughout Europe. They are often places of both majesty and tranquility.

I will never forget entering the synagogue in Budapest, Hungary, for the first time. Its towering walls and ornate beauty made me forget the world outside and opened my ears

[1] Abraham Joshua Heschel, *The Sabbath*, (New York: Noonday Press, 1951), 8, 21.
[2] Ibid., 9.
[3] Ibid.

to the divine. The Sabbath provides a similar respite at the end of every week. But it is a *cathedral of time,* as Heschel writes, rather than simply space. We find a sense of rest and stillness that makes the Sabbath a sacred refuge.

As a wife and parent, I understand the gift of time—what it means to spend a day leisurely with my husband or daughter in pursuit of nothing more than recreation and relationship. It is a great treasure.

On one occasion, my daughter asked me to come and sit on her bed just to visit. I realized that all she wanted was my time—a few minutes focused on her alone. That simple request spoke deep truth. My money and other gifts just weren't enough. She needed time with me alone. I felt bad—even ashamed—that she had to ask for it, but I learned an important lesson that day.

In a similar way, God asks for our time through Sabbath. In return, He restores and strengthens our spirits, souls, and bodies through the hours spent with Him.

# CHAPTER 16

# An Eternal Covenant

THE TORAH[1] DESCRIBES *Shabbat* as an eternal covenant between God and the Jewish people. The gift of time was so important to God and his people that it became an enduring agreement:

> "So *Bnei-Yisrael* is to keep the *Shabbat,* to observe the *Shabbat* throughout their generations as a perpetual covenant. It is a sign between Me and *Bnei-Yisrael* forever, for in six days *ADONAI* made heaven and earth, and on the seventh day He ceased from the work and rested" (Exodus 31:16–17 TLV).

There is compensation for keeping the Sabbath holy:

> "If you turn back your foot from *Shabbat,*
> from doing your pleasure on My holy day,
> and call *Shabbat* a delight,
> the holy day of *ADONAI* honorable,
> If you honor it, not going your own ways,
> not seeking your own pleasure,
> nor speaking your usual speech,
> then You will delight yourself in *ADONAI,*
> and I will let you ride over the heights of the earth,
> I will feed you with the heritage of your father Jacob."
> For the mouth of *ADONAI* has spoken (Isaiah 58:13–14 TLV).

---

[1] The first five books of the Old Testament, considered to be the books of Moses.

Sabbath observance is considered a universal day of adoration and reverence:

> "And it will come to pass,
>   that from one New Moon to another,
>   and from one *Shabbat* to another,
>   all flesh will come to bow down before Me,"
> says ADONAI (Isaiah 66:23 TLV).

The glory of Jerusalem corresponded to the Jews keeping the Sabbath:

> "However, if you listen attentively to Me," says ADONAI, "to bring in no burden through the gates of this city on *Yom Shabbat*, but sanctify *Yom Shabbat* and do no work on it, then there will enter in through the gates of this city kings and princes sitting on the throne of David, riding in chariots and on horses—with their princes, the people of Judah and those dwelling in Jerusalem—and this city will be inhabited forever ... But if you do not listen to Me to keep *Yom Shabbat* holy, by not bearing a burden or entering through the gates of Jerusalem on *Yom Shabbat*, then I will set its gates on fire, and it will consume the citadels of Jerusalem, and not be quenched" (Jeremiah 17:24–27 TLV).

God reproved Israel for its continued disregard of the Sabbath:

> So I led them out from the land of Egypt and brought them into the wilderness. I gave them My laws and taught them My judgments, which if a man does, he will live by them. I also gave them My *Shabbatot*, as a sign between Me and them, so that they would know that I am ADONAI who made them holy.
>
> But the house of Israel rebelled against Me in the wilderness. They did not walk in My statutes. They rejected My judgments,

which if a man does, he will live by them. They greatly profaned My *Shabbatot*. Then I resolved to pour out My fury on them in the wilderness to consume them (Ezekiel 20:10–13 TLV).

# CHAPTER 17

# Compared to a Bride

THE SABBATH IS also compared to a bride, coming to the people of God in purity and sanctity. Many *Shabbat* rituals surround this thought. Sixteenth-century mystics created the Friday evening service called in Hebrew *Kabbalat Shabbat,* which means welcoming the Sabbath. The song *L'kah Dodi* is often sung as part of the liturgy:

> Come my beloved to meet the Bride.
> Let us welcome the presence of the Sabbath
> Come in peace ... and come in joy ...
> Come, O Bride! Come, O Bride!

Today, in Jewish Orthodox settings, as the last verse of the song is sung, the congregation will turn away from the ark housing the *Torah* and bow before the synagogue entrance as if the Bride of *Shabbat* were about to enter.

As believers, the idea of Sabbath as a pure bride finds a home in our hearts at the end of Leviticus 23:3, for *it is for a Sabbath to the Lord.* We hold close and yet see beyond the Orthodox view of Sabbath being the bride, as we embrace the New Covenant[1] idea that we, the church, have become that pure Bride by *Yeshua's* blood. Therefore, we greet the Sabbath

---

[1] New Testament.

prepared to steal away with our beloved Bridegroom for twenty-four hours. *Shabbat* is a weekly honeymoon with the Bridegroom, and it is a glimpse of what it will be like to be with the Lord forever.

Rather than becoming paralyzed by rules, the Sabbath should evoke great joy and expectation, as a bride would have on her wedding day. As Messiah's Bride, we are being presented to God as righteous and without spot or blemish (Ephesians 5:27). We set apart the time of *Shabbat* to be alone with our Bridegroom in delightful exclusivity. Scripture contains many beautiful pictures of the Bride and Bridegroom captivated by each other in the bond of love. Song of Songs describes in detail the intimate relationship between the Bride and Bridegroom. Song of Songs speaks of the Bride coming up from the wilderness leaning on her beloved (Song of Songs 8:5).

Judaism fully embraces the idea of Israel as the Bride being prepared for the one and only true God. Hosea describes the suffering and depth of love that God has for His wayward Bride. She strayed far from her lover and husband and became a prostitute, and yet the heavenly Bridegroom wooed her back and loved her utterly despite the heartache suffered because of her rejection and betrayal.

The same message of boundless love resounds throughout Scripture. And it may be most clearly seen in the New Covenant where Jesus reached out to the woman caught in adultery. This woman, who deserved to die according to the Law, is a definitive example of the rebellious and ungrateful Bride, who is captivated and eventually changed by a loving and forgiving Bridegroom.

As the romance story of the ages unfolds, we recognize that the Bridegroom is the Lamb who was sacrificed for humanity's sin. Gary Wiens writes in his book *Bridal Intercession:*

You see, the so-called fairy tales of history really are true. The prince really has kissed the girl, the humble handmaid really is the Princess, and the Beauty who has been under the spell of the poison apple really will be brought to life. The King will have his glorious Bride and the desires of His heart will be satisfied. The stories are clear and you'll find them throughout Scripture. Our God is a God of love, and His burning heart is the heart of a Bridegroom Who will not be dissuaded from His task. His zeal burns for the restoration of His people, and He will not relent until the broken woman, whose name is Jerusalem, shines forth in the way He intended, as a praise in all the earth (Isaiah 62:7).[1]

Can it be, in these last days as the Church anticipates the Lord's return, that the keeping of *Shabbat* will be restored to the whole body of Messiah as a foretaste of the redeemed Bride's glorious reunion with the bridegroom?

As Gentile believers who love Israel, we invite Jews whom we meet in our everyday world to our *Shabbat* table in celebration. They accept our invitations and often become renewed in their love for their Jewish roots, open to the message of Messiah, and even "jealous" that we celebrate the Sabbath. Could these evening meals together between Jew and Gentile—at the table lit with Sabbath lights and filled with *Yeshua's* love—be a sample of something that we celebrate together in eternity? That is our hope.

---

[1] Gary Wiens, *Bridal Intercession,* (Rockville, Missouri: Oasis House, 2001), 35.

# CHAPTER 18

# Renewal and Relaxation

WHAT SHOULD THE Sabbath look like for us today?
Daniel Juster writes:

> The pages of the New Testament do not at all contradict the sense
> of the Sabbath given in the Tenach. Nor does *Yeshua* break the
> Sabbath in its true sense. He calls Himself 'Lord of the Sabbath'...
> Messianic Jews must avoid a legalistic approach to Sabbath, where
> rules are imposed ad infinitum. However, if Sabbath is to be taken
> seriously, there are some basic principles, which may be applied by
> our people.[1]

We set aside a day for the remembrance and celebration
of *Shabbat*. This day is free from work and the burdens of
day-to-day living. It represents an act of faith in which we stop
our worldly efforts, and allow the Creator to meet our needs
abundantly. This day should be a time of renewal, relaxation,
and joy. Many recreational choices are possible for the remembrance of *Shabbat:* reading, taking walks, enjoying nature, and
giving time to family and friends. Since Scripture states the
Sabbath is for the Lord, could it be that we should spend some
of the time in reflection of Him alone?

[1] Daniel Juster, *Jewish Roots*, (Rockville, Maryland: DAVAR Publishing Co,
1986), 197, 199.

CHAPTER 19

# Intercessory Purposes

I CANNOT EMPHASIZE enough the importance of prayer and intercession for believers. Through the centuries, God has used prayer warriors to fight for His truth on earth. Abraham cried out to God on behalf of Sodom, even though he knew the city was full of sin; God answered his prayer. Moses pleaded for Israel, even offering his own life; God heard and honored his cries. Habakkuk asked God to right injustice, and Nehemiah dreamed about and interceded for the rebuilding of the temple and the restoration of Sabbath-keeping for the ancient Hebrews, who had already forgotten their significance.

*Yeshua* stands as the supreme example of intercession, earnestly pleading the cause of His people. He requested mercy for those who hated and betrayed Him, even the thief on the cross next to Him. The life of *Yeshua* became a living representation of intercession because he was perfect, pure, and sinless. He obeyed the Father at all times, and took time to be alone with Him. He found sanctuary and the gift of time in the Lord's presence. There, He rested and received rejuvenation. And He prayed for the lost sheep of the House of Israel.

Today, God still calls His Bride to intercede in prayer for lost and hurting people. Gary Wiens speaks of the place of the Bride in this context:

In the prophetic portrait called the book of Esther, he is inviting us to approach intercession through the doorway of romance, to dial up all His daring and passionate emotions, to tell Him all over again that we say 'yes' to His proposals, that we choose Him again even as at the first. He wants us to presume upon His grace and mercy, to enter the Holy of Holies with confident boldness, knowing that His scepter or righteousness is extended toward us at all times, because he is a King in love, and we are His bride![1]

As the Bride of Messiah, we fulfill God's intercessory purposes on earth when we keep Sabbath. Sabbath serves as a prophetic call to Israel, as God's people repeat it throughout the ages. Sabbath demonstrates that God has made a covenant with his people and that He will keep it. Sabbath is an act of intercessory prayer that resounds into eternity. It is language that we hear without words, yet voiced through our actions. Sabbath stands forever as a sign between God and humanity. God shows in word and deed that He is our provider and physical and spiritual Sabbath rest are available for those who will seek it. The observance and remembrance of Sabbath reinforce these truths in a real and weekly manifestation.

For Israel, the Sabbath is a sign that God has kept His promises to her and will continue keeping them until *Yeshua* comes again. As Messianic believers enter into the Sabbath rest, the act itself becomes an intercessory call for the light of *Yeshua* to shine into the darkness, illuminating the hearts of Jews around the world to the truth of salvation through no one else but Him.

[1] Wiens, *Bridal Intercession*, 95.

An invitation to Sabbath rest rings throughout the universe as God's people strike the first match to light the Sabbath candles, lift the brimming cup of wine, and bless the God of Israel on the evening that is separated unto the Bridegroom and Bride alone.

# CHAPTER 20

# Ritually Set Apart

SABBATH'S SPIRITUAL SIGNIFICANCE is seen most clearly as
we are ritually set apart and begin with a festive Friday evening
meal—a special event that reminds us that we are keeping
covenant with God and entering into a holy time. To believers
in Messiah, *Shabbat* is a foretaste of the Marriage Supper of the
Lamb, when Messiah's Bride unites with her beloved in heaven
because of the blood sacrifice of *Yeshua* (Revelation 19:7).

The Jewish dispersion created variation in Sabbath rituals
as God's people scattered after the destruction of the Temple
in AD 70. God's Word does not specify how to conduct the
evening *Shabbat* meal, so many traditions exist.

Most Sabbath traditions are interpretations of the Law
by Jewish rabbis. Rabbis and scholars debated for centuries
the manner and customs for honoring the Sabbath. They
carved out many traditions, which are a blessing to keep, but
we should not consider their observance as equal to biblical
obedience. We should distinguish between the scriptural
and the rabbinical when integrating Sabbath practices into
our homes. Honoring the Sabbath and keeping it holy should
reflect the biblical intent. In the following appendices, v
find a suggested Messianic Sabbath evening liturgy gu
history for its observance.

In Jewish observance, all days begin and end in the evening. *Shabbat* and festival days are the same, beginning and ending at twilight or sundown.

# Messianic Jewish Sabbath Traditions and Prayers

*Six days a week we wrestle with the world,*
*wringing profit from the earth; on the Sabbath,*
*we especially care for the seed of eternity planted in the soul.*

—*Abraham Joshua Heschel*

## Table

If you want to make the celebration of *Shabbat* in your home special and memorable, invite friends, use a special tablecloth and dishes, eat in the dining room rather than the kitchen, and put freshly cut flowers on the table. Each of these simple acts symbolically changes the rhythm of the week. Traditionally, a white tablecloth is used on *Shabbat* to signify the holiness and purity of a bride.

Ritual objects are a wonderful way to create the ambience of *Shabbat*. Use objects that you already have at home or purchase the specific Judaica designed for *Shabbat*.

You will need:

- Candlesticks (at least two)
- *Challah* cover (a table linen or napkin to cover the Sabbath bread)
- *Kiddush* cup (a wine glass)

## Food and Dress

Since the *Shabbat* meal is the most elaborate meal of the week, participants should wear special attire. Clothing varies from family to family. Some wear special robes of satin or silk; elegant, yet emphasizing comfort. Others dress up completely. In Israel, where attire is usually very casual, *Shabbat* meal may mean wearing white instead of colored clothing. Among the Jewish Orthodox in Israel, Sabbath is a very dressy affair. The key is to find a dress style that is special, yet comfortable for your family.

*Shabbat* food should be distinctive as well. It should include *challah* (Sabbath bread) and wine or grape juice. In most homes, many specially prepared dishes are used, separating this meal from the routine of the week, including a special dessert. *Shabbat* recipe suggestions are included in this book. Many people cook enough food to last for the next day as well.

## Candle Lighting (*Hadlakat Nerot*)

Lighting *Shabbat* candles on Friday as evening approaches marks the beginning of the Sabbath. Candlelighting reminds us of the light that dawned at creation when God said in the Genesis, the first book of the *Torah, "Let there be light."* As Messianic believers, we also remember that *Yeshua* is the light of the world who shines in the darkness.

Traditionally, two candles are lit, representing the two times the *Torah* cites the Fourth Commandment. Some believe that the two Sabbath candles symbolize that Jews must "remember," or *zachor* (Exodus 20:8) and "observe," or *shamor* (Deuteronomy 5:12) the Sabbath day. Others say the two candles represent God and creation or God and redemption. All of these are beautiful symbols and good reasons to light the candles of *Shabbat*.

*Shabbat* candles serve at least two real purposes: they lend light to the Sabbath table and add an element of harmony for the Friday evening meal. They also symbolize the light of gladness, which *Shabbat* provides us.

The candles should be lit where the meal will be eaten and where all may enjoy them until they burn out. Other candles may be added. Some families light a candle for every child. Some use a *menorah* and light all seven branches.

*Shabbat* officially begins with the lighting of the candles. Traditionally, they are lit at 6:00 pm or when three stars appear outside. Ultra-Orthodox Jews use candle-lighting time schedules found on Jewish websites or calendars, usually specifying them to be lit at least 18 minutes before sunset. The times are calculated down to the minute before sunset to avoid the labor of lighting them after *Shabbat* begins.

Most Messianic Jewish believers light the candles after everyone arrives and just before the beginning of the meal. Usually, women light the two candles, but anyone may light them.

If a woman is married, she covers her head in reverence. She makes three big sweeps over the candles after lighting them. This act symbolizes her desire for light, rest, and peace to enter her home on *Shabbat*. She covers her eyes and repeats the prayer below. After the prayer, the woman opens her eyes and she first sees the warm Sabbath lights. These lights represent the rest and harmony she has diligently worked to create by preparing her home and family for this special time.

## Traditional Prayer

*Baruch Atah Adonai, Eloheinu, Melech haolam asher kidishanu b'mitz'votav v'tzivanu l'had'lik ner shel Shabbat.*

*Blessed are you, O Lord our God, King of the universe, who has sanctified us and inspired us to kindle the Sabbath lights.*

## Messianic Prayer

*Baruch Atah Adonai, Eloheinu, Melech haolam, asher kidishanu b'dam Yeshua v'tzivanu l'hiot or l'goyim.*

*Blessed are you, O Lord our God, Ruler of the universe, who sanctifies us by the blood of Yeshua and inspires us to be a light to the nations.*

The woman may offer a spontaneous prayer from her heart, thanking God for *Yeshua,* the light of the world. She may also remember the Jewish people around the world who are celebrating *Shabbat*:

May Yeshua be revealed as they keep the covenant of *Shabbat* between God and his people in their homes, and may the true light of God through *Yeshua,* shine into their hearts.

## Hand Washing (*Netilat Yadayim*)

Many people around the world wash their hands before meals as a matter of cleanliness and health. The Jewish people, however, were likely the first to institutionalize laws for hand washing. They were years ahead of most people groups in understanding that diseases were transmitted from person to person by unclean hands.

The hand washing tradition symbolically underscores that the *Shabbat* meal is a holy, spiritual event. Participants wash by using a pitcher and bowl and pouring water from the pitcher over one hand and then the other. Then the bowl and pitcher are passed from one person to another until everyone has had a turn. A small towel is passed as well.

Spiritually, the hand-washing experience allows time and opportunity to enter the *Shabbat* with clean hands and a pure heart.

> *Who may go up on the mountain of* ADONAI?
> *Who may stand in His holy place?*
> *One with clean hands and a pure heart,*
> *who has not lifted his soul in vain,*
> *nor sworn deceitfully (Psalm 24:3–4 TLV).*

It is by the blood of Yeshua that our hearts and hands become clean.

> *If we confess our sins, He is faithful and righteous to forgive our sins and purify us from all unrighteousness (1 John 1:9 TLV).*

Hand washing in Hebrew also speaks to dedication. This act affords participants the opportunity to dedicate the work of their hands completely to the Lord and His kingdom.

## Traditional and Messianic Prayer

*Baruch Atah Adonai Eloheinu, Melech haolam asher kidishanu b'mitz'votav bietzeevanu al netilat yadayim.*

*Blessed are You, O Lord our God, Ruler of the universe who has sanctified us by your commandments and inspired us to wash hands.*

## Recited in Unison (Messianic response)

*I dedicate my hands to Yeshua, the Messiah, to serve him only.*

## Blessing the Children (*Birkat HaYeladim*)

The Place of Blessing

Blessings from the head of the home to the children and wife are a significant part of *Shabbat* tradition. God originally planned for community life to focus on family. *Shabbat* is the time to unite, yet set ourselves apart from the world. *Shabbat* is a sanctified time in which we can recapture what we often lose during the hectic week. Our weekday obligations often reflect what we do rather than who we are. When our family sits together over a *Shabbat* meal, or spends part of the *Shabbat* relaxing or reflecting on God, we rekindle the awe we experienced in our first love relationship with *Yeshua*. We take time to focus on family and friends with greater enthusiasm. This time *set apart* allows us to recreate ourselves in His presence as we prepare for the new week.

While we often feel loving thoughts for our children, we don't always express them aloud. Offering a blessing from our hearts over our children is a beautiful *Shabbat* tradition that can create lifelong memories. Spoken blessings have the power to inspire our children to higher living; they also protect them under the wings of unconditional love along the journey. Some parents and grandparents compose their own blessings for their children, acknowledging something they did that week or affirming a child's special gifts. This time is perfect for emphasizing the strength and growth of character displayed in a child's life.

Some Jewish fathers who own a *tallit,* or Jewish prayer shawl, use them during this portion of the Sabbath celebration meal. When a Jewish man puts on a prayer shawl, he recites this psalm found in Jewish prayer books:

> *How precious is Your love, O God!*
> *The children of men find refuge in the shadow of Your wings*
> *(Psalm 36:8 TLV).*

A father understands the powerful imagery conveyed when he wraps himself in his *tallit* and opens the four corners of it to bring his children close to his side for his blessing. The Hebrew word for the corner of the *tallit* is *canaph,* or wing. The tassels on the corners of the *tallit* are called *tzitzit*, which symbolize the *Torah* or the commandments of God.

Before repeating the blessing, the father may cover his head and shoulders with his *tallit* and call the children to stand next to him to be folded under his wings. The children receive a wonderful image of God's wings protecting and guarding them through their father's wisdom and leadership. Ultimately, this is a picture of God Himself as a protector and His Word as a guide.

## For Girls

*Y'simeikh Elohim k'Sara, Rivka, Rachel, Leah, Miriam, v' Elisheva.*

*May God make you like Sarah, Rebekah, Rachel, Leah, Mary, and Elizabeth.*

## For Boys

*Y'simeikh Elohim k'Ephraim, Menashe, Yochanan, Mattai, v' Stefen.*

*May God make you like Ephraim, Manasseh, John, Matthew, and Stephen.*

# Blessing Over the Wife (*Birkat HaEeshah*)

The father and the children stand in honor while the mother remains seated. They recite from the book of Proverbs.

*An accomplished woman who can find?*
*Her value is far beyond rubies.*
*Her husband's heart trusts in her,*
*and he lacks nothing valuable.*
*She brings him good and not harm*
*all the days of her life.*
*She selects wool and flax*
*and her hands work willingly.*
*She is like merchant ships,*
*bringing her sustenance from afar.*
*She rises while it is still night*
*and provides food for her household*

*and portions for her servant girls.*
*She considers a field and buys it.*
*From the fruit of her hands she plants a vineyard.*
*She girds herself with strength*
*and invigorates her arms.*
*She discerns that her business is good.*
*Her lamp never goes out at night.*
*She extends her hands to the spindle*
*and her palm grasps the spinning wheel.*
*She spreads out her palms to the poor,*
*and extends her hands to the needy.*
*She is not afraid of snow for her house,*
*for her whole household is clothed in scarlet wool.*
*She makes her own luxurious coverings.*
*Her clothing is fine linen and purple.*
*Her husband is respected at the city gates,*
*when he sits among the elders of the land.*
*She makes linen garments and sells them*
*and supplies sashes to the merchants.*
*Strength and dignity are her clothing,*
*and she laughs at the days to come.*
*She opens her mouth with wisdom—*
*a lesson of kindness is on her tongue.*
*She watches over the affairs of her household,*
*and does not eat the bread of idleness.*
*Her children arise and bless her,*
*her husband also praises her:*
*"Many daughters have excelled,*
*but you surpass them all."*
*Charm is deceitful and beauty is vain,*
*but a woman who fears* ADONAI *will be praised.*

*Give her the fruit of her hands.*
*Let her deeds be her praise at the gates (Proverbs 31:10–31 TLV).*

After the recitation of this proverb, the father places his hands on his wife and prays a prayer of blessing and gratitude from his heart. The children remain standing as he prays.

## Blessing over the Wine (*Kiddush*)

*Kiddush* is derived from the Hebrew word *kadosh,* or holy. The reciting of the *Kiddush* precedes the Sabbath meal; it is the sanctification of *Shabbat* over the wine. In Jewish life, wine is a symbol for joy. The *Kiddush* describes *Shabbat* as a commemoration of both the universal, the creation of the world, and the particular, God's redemption of Israel from Egypt. Ultimately, it symbolizes God's greatest gift to the Jewish people and all humanity—the blood sacrifice of *Yeshua.*

While wine often symbolizes the blood sacrifice of *Yeshua,* the passing of the *Kiddush* cup during the *Shabbat* meal is not necessarily reminiscent of the Lord's Supper, which is commemorated with unleavened bread during Passover. Although many believers cannot lift this cup without remembering the precious and life-giving sacrifice of *Yeshua,* it is generally not considered communion. The *Shabbat* table is to be a table of joy, similar to the celebration the bride and bridegroom enjoy on their special day. Therefore, the *Kiddush* cup at the Sabbath table is lifted high with a blessing to the God of Abraham, Isaac, and Jacob, symbolizing exuberance and gladness to all.

*"I am the vine, you are the branches. He who abides in Me, and I in Him bears much fruit" (John 15:5 NKJV).*

Traditional and Messianic Prayer

*Baruch Atah Adonai Eloheinu, Melech haolam boray pre hagafen.*
*Amen.*

*Blessed are You, O Lord our God, Ruler of the universe who*
*creates the fruit of the vine. Amen.*

After the father says the blessing and drinks, he passes a
common *Kiddush* cup around the table. Males drink in birth
order, females drink in birth order, and lastly the children
drink in birth order. This practice gives respect to those who
are older. If a gathering is too large to use a common chalice,
then individuals may lift their wine glasses in unison to partake
after the blessing.

## Blessing over the Bread (*HaMotzi Lechem*)

In Jewish history, *challah* (bread) symbolizes *manna*, the
special food that God provided for the Israelites during their
years of wandering in the desert. Traditionally, the Sabbath
table includes two loaves, because God provided enough *manna*
on the sixth day for the seventh.

*Challah* is an essential part of the meal. Some Messianic
communities fast on Friday until the *Shabbat* meal, making the
first bite of bread extra delicious and meaningful.

*Challah* is a sweet bread made with egg and considered richer
than everyday bread. In pre-Holocaust times throughout the
former Soviet Union and Europe, Jews considered egg bread
a food for the wealthy. Sugar or honey was added to make the
*challah* even more special.

The *challah* is made with three or more strands to create a braid for several reasons. The three strands symbolize the commands to observe *Shabbat* found in the Ten Commandments. One strand represents the word *zachar,* or to "remember." A second strand represents the word *shomar,* or to "guard." The third strand is for *b'dibbur echad,* which represents the words "spoken as one" or that these commands of "remember" and "guard" become one unit. Finally, the *Shabbat* signifies and reminds us of three different epochs: the creation of the world, the Exodus from Egypt, and the Messianic era.

Fancy braided breads, created with four or more strands, may be used for Jewish High Holy Days or weddings. On the Jewish New Year, *Rosh HaShana,* the braided *challah* is formed into a circle representing eternity or the circle of life. Sometimes golden raisins are baked with the bread to make it sweeter and more festive. Poppy seeds or sesame seeds may be baked on top.

Although a knife is placed on the table at *Shabbat,* it is not used to cut the *challah.* The Bible recounts the time God tested the patriarch Abraham, who did not use a knife on his son, Isaac. Instead, God provided a ram. Therefore, the bread is torn and not cut.

A saltshaker is also placed near the bread and the father sprinkles salt on the bread before he passes it around the table. The salt commemorates several things:

1.  The salty tears of bondage in Egypt or our bondage to sin.
2.  That a covenant ratified by salt is everlasting.
3.  That as believers we are to be salt in this decaying world.

## Traditional and Messianic Prayer

*Baruch Atah Adonai Eloheinu Melech haolam hamotzi lechem min haaretz. Amen.*

*Blessed are You, O Lord our God, Ruler of the universe who gives us bread from the earth. Amen.*

After the blessing, the father sprinkles salt on one loaf of bread, breaks it in half, pinches one bite to eat, and passes it around the table. Everyone pinches a bite to eat.

# The Meal

The meal is a time to linger over good food and to enjoy conversation and company. Every person should be included in the conversation, making everyone feel important. The father takes the initiative to hear something from everyone, including the guests at the table. This is the perfect opportunity to follow the New Covenant directive to rejoice with those who rejoice and weep with those who weep (Romans 12:15), as the father asks each person about the joys and disappointments of the week. This intimate fellowship bridges the gap between the aloof callousness of the world and the desperate need to rejoice in each other's victories and bear one another's burdens. This simple act of dialogue over the meal enables families and friends to grow closer.

# After the Meal

Traditions of after-dinner activities vary from home to home. In the Gateways Beyond Messianic Community in Cyprus, everyone participates in a group activity that engages both children and adults. These activities require some creativity, but they can top the evening off with spice and laughter. A family might view a movie or read a book together—a few chapters at a time over several Shabbats. The key is to do something together that will bring the family closer. It might include simple conversation or doing something special that includes the children.

## The Sabbath Day

Have a festive midday meal on the Sabbath, preferably requiring little effort to prepare. Serve leftovers from the evening meal, or prepare cold salads and meats ahead. The key is not to spend the day in the kitchen, thus losing the joy of Sabbath rest. Again, *Kiddush* is recited over the wine or grape juice. After lunch, many people take an opportunity for a long and luxurious nap, catch up on some reading, take a long walk, or anything that enriches and restores the soul, body, and spirit. Some spend the day reading God's Word, listening to worship music, and enjoying His presence.

### Havdalah

*Havdalah* means "separation" in Hebrew. This practice brings *Shabbat* to a close in the same way it began—with light. For this ritual, use one braided candle instead of two separate candles. The braided candles symbolize the two separate flames becoming one through the unifying force of *Shabbat*. Again, we can see a picture of God and His Bride coming together. This ceremony includes blessings over the wine, spices, and light.

The aromatic spices remind us that the Sabbath is going out with sweetness and the remembrance of having rested. As the Bride of Messiah, the Sabbath ends with the warmth of having lingered in the company of our Bridegroom, *Yeshua*. The candles are extinguished with a drop of wine, reminding us again of the pleasantness and joy of Sabbath as it comes to an end. We are now ready to greet another week.

# Sabbath Songs

*The seventh day sings. An old allegory asserts: When Adam*
*saw the majesty of the Sabbath, its greatness and glory,*
*and the joy it conferred upon all beings, he intoned*
*a song of praise for the Sabbath day as if to give thanks*
*to the Sabbath day. Then God said to him: Thou singest a song*
*of praise to the Sabbath day, and singest none to Me, the God of the*
*Sabbath? Thereupon the Sabbath rose from its seat,*
*and prostrated herself before God, saying; It is a good thing*
*to give thanks unto the Lord. And the whole of creation added:*
*And to sing praise unto Thy Name, O Most High.*

—*Berthold Auerbach*

AFTER THE BLESSINGS comes a good time to sing songs of
joy pertaining to our salvation or our joy in coming to the
Sabbath to rest.

Found in the Hebrew verb to pray, *l'hitpallel*, we see more
than to make petitions to God about our daily needs. It
means to reflect upon our lives. We are commanded to pray
in Psalm 50:15 and I Thessalonians 5:17. We pray at various
times—during affliction and joyful times with gratitude. It is
personal and corporate. In Jewish culture, many gatherings
include prayer as a community like circumcisions, weddings,
holidays, and Sabbaths.

Prayer at the Sabbath table is especially important. As the Sabbath day is set apart, prayer elevates the gathering to the realm of holy, as a family or group declares corporately that the God of heaven and earth as Creator who is intimately involved in our lives. There are several famous, traditional Jewish songs for Sabbath that are a way to bless the Lord of Israel and each other around the Sabbath table.

*Shalom Aleichem:*
*Heveinu shalom Aleichem (3x)*
*Heveinu shalom, shalom, shalom Aleichem*
*We bring peace upon you. We bring peace, peace, peace upon you.*

*Shabbat Shalom:*
*Shabbat Shalom, Shabbat Shalom,*
*Shabbat, Shabbat, Shabbat, Shabbat Shalom*
*Shabbat Shabbat Shabbat Shabbat Shalom (2x)*
*Shabbat Shalom, Shabbat Shalom,*
*Shabbat, Shabbat, Shabbat, Shabbat Shalom.*
*Sabbath Peace.*

*Sabbath Peace:*
*Oseh Shalom bimromav*
*Hu ya'asay shalom aleinoo*
*Ve'al kol Yisrael*
*V'imru imru amen (repeat)*
*Ya'asay shalom, ya'say shalom*
*Shalom aleinoo ve'al kol Yisrael (2x)*
*He who makes peace in His high places makes peace for all of Israel and say amen.*

*Am Yisrael Chai:*
*Am Yisrael Chai, am Yisrael chai*
*Am Yisrael, am Yisrael, am Yisrael chai (repeat)*
*Ode avinu chai, ode Avinu chai*
*Ode avinu, ode Avinu, ode avinu chai (repeat)*
*The people of Israel live. Our Father still lives.*

The *Sh'ma* is a traditional prayer spoken daily by Jewish people around the world. It has been adapted as a declaration of faith for believers in Messiah, *Yeshua*. When proclaimed in faith, it is an intercession for the salvation of all of Israel.

*Sh'ma:*
*Sh'ma Yisrael Adonai Eloheinu Adonai Echad*
*Baruch Shem k'vod malchooto l'olam va'ed*
*Yeshua hu ha-Mashiach hu Adon ha-kol. (added by Messianic*
*believers, not a part of the original Sh'ma.)*
*Hear O Israel, the Lord our God, the Lord is One. Blessed be the*
*name of His glorious kingdom forever and ever. Yeshua, he is the*
*Messiah, He is Lord of all.*

*Aaronic Benediction:*
*Y'va-rech'cha Adonai, v'yeesh-ma reh-cha*
*Y'ayr Adonai panahv ey-lecha vee-choo-nencha*
*Y'sa Adonai panahv ey-lecha v'yah-sem l'cha*
*Shalom*

*"The Lord bless you and keep you;*
*The Lord make his face shine upon you,*
*And be gracious to you;*
*The Lord lift up his countenance upon you,*
*and give you peace (Numbers 6:23–26 NKJV).*

# Sabbath Recipes

*"All Jewish communities incorporate foods mentioned in the Bible—*
*such as almonds, apples, dates, raisins, and honey—*
*as symbolic ingredients in festival dishes."*

—*Gil Marks*

## Creamy White Bean and Rosemary Soup for Sabbath

This hearty winter soup is a wonderful start to a *Shabbat*
meal. Its creamy white color is another appropriate welcome
for the Bride and Bridegroom on *Shabbat.*

- 2, 15 oz. cans cannelloni beans, drained and rinsed
- 3 white onions, chopped
- 1 clove garlic, finely minced
- 2 branches fresh rosemary
- 1/4 cup butter
- 2 quarts low-sodium chicken stock
- 1/2 cup chopped green onions for garnish
- Salt and pepper to taste
- Dash cayenne powder for garnish

Sauté onions with butter until translucent. Add garlic and cook for a couple more minutes, being careful not to burn the garlic. Add the white beans, rosemary, and chicken stock. Cover and bring to a boil, then reduce heat and simmer for 30 minutes. Remove the rosemary. Allow to cool and use handheld food emulsifier to blend until creamy. Add salt and pepper and stir. Garnish each bowl with a dash of cayenne powder and sprinkle with chopped green onions.

# Roast Chicken with Orange Glaze

- 1 roasting chicken, 4 to 5 pounds
- Seasoning salt
- 1 onion, peeled and halved
- 1 carrot, cut in 1-inch chunks
- 1 rib celery, cut in 1-inch chunks
- 1 tablespoon cornstarch
- 1 cup orange juice
- Finely chopped green onion and parsley, for garnish

Wash chicken and rub with seasoning salt. Stuff the cavity with onion, carrot, and celery. Place chicken in shallow baking dish or on a rack in a roasting pan. Roast at 325 degrees for about three hours. Mix orange juice and cornstarch in a small bowl or measuring cup. About thirty minutes before chicken is done, brush chicken generously with orange juice mixture. Brush again about fifteen minutes before done. Sprinkle with chopped green onion and parsley before serving. Whole roasted chicken serves six.

# Shabbat Couscous

- 1/2 cup butter
- 1 1/3 cup couscous (wheat-grain semolina)
- 1 small onion, chopped
- 3 green onions, chopped
- 1 cup chicken broth or bouillon
- Salt and pepper to taste

Melt butter and sauté onion until softened; add couscous and sauté another two minutes, stirring constantly. Add green onion and sauté one minute. Heat broth or bouillon in a separate saucepan; stir hot broth or bouillon into couscous and vegetables. Add salt and pepper to taste. Cover and let sit for five minutes. Stir with fork. Serves six.

# Sabbath Tzimmes (Stew)

- 6 medium carrots, sliced
- 1 large sweet potato, cubed
- 1 T butter
- 1 T real maple syrup, plus 2 tsp brown sugar
- 1/4 cup orange juice
- 1 tsp orange zest
- Dash salt
- 3 slices pineapple, cut into chunks
- 1/4 tsp nutmeg

Melt butter in saucepan and add carrots. Cook on low flame for 10–15 minutes. Add sweet potato, maple syrup, brown sugar, orange juice, and salt. Cook over low heat for 20–30 minutes until carrots and potato are tender. Add pineapple, orange zest, and nutmeg. Serve warm.

# Mandarin and Almond Green Salad

- 1 medium red onion, thinly sliced into rings
- 2 cups torn romaine or green leaf lettuce
- 1 can mandarin oranges, drained
- 1 cup slivered almonds

# Red Wine Vinaigrette

- 1/3 cup olive oil
- 3 tablespoons red wine vinegar
- 1/2 teaspoon salt
- Dash pepper

Slice onion into thin rings. Toss with lettuce, mandarin pieces, and almonds. Combine vinaigrette ingredients and whisk well. Toss with salad in a serving bowl. Green salad recipe serves six.

# Hannah's Festive Honey Cake

- 1 cup sugar
- 3 cups self-rising flour
- 1 1/2 teaspoon cinnamon
- 1/4 teaspoon ground cloves
- 1 teaspoon ground nutmeg
- 1 cup honey
- 1 cup strong coffee
- 3/4 cup coconut oil
- 1 teaspoon vanilla extract
- 2 eggs
- 1/2 cup semisweet chocolate morsels (optional)
- 1/2 cup pecans (optional)
- 1/2 cup shredded coconut

Preheat to 350 degrees F. Spray a Bundt pan with non-stick vegetable spray. In a large mixing bowl, combine flour, sugar, cinnamon, cloves, and nutmeg; make a well in the center. Add honey, coffee, oil, vanilla, and eggs; beat until well blended and smooth. Stir in chocolate morsels, shredded coconut, and pecans. Pour into prepared Bundt pan. Bake forty-five to sixty minutes or until a tester inserted in the center comes out clean. Cool in Bundt pan for twenty minutes. Remove from Bundt pan; cool completely on a wire rack.

# Challah (Sabbath Bread)

- 1/2 cup oil
- 1 cup honey
- 1 tablespoon salt
- 4 eggs
- 3 packages dried yeast, dissolved in 1 cup warm (75–120 degrees) water
- 2 cups additional warm water
- 8–10 cups flour

Mix the ingredients, putting the oil into the bowl first and then measure and add the honey, using the same measuring cup in which you measured the oil. This little trick allows the honey to run smoothly out of the measuring cup. Add the remaining ingredients in the order given.

Knead for approximately ten minutes and transfer the dough into an oiled bowl.

Let the dough rise in a large bowl that has been coated with oil. When transferring the dough into the oiled bowl, be sure to turn it on all sides so that it gets a thin coating of oil. Place the bowl in a warm place until the dough is double in size, punch it down, and knead a bit more.

Place the dough back in the bowl and let it rise a second time. This should take about one hour. Punch down and cut into sizes desired. For two medium loaves, divide into six strands. Make two loaves of three-braided strands. When the breads are shaped, brush them generously with egg yolk, melted butter, and honey, and sprinkle either poppy seeds or sesame seeds on the loaves. Bake in 350 degree oven for approximately 25–30 minutes or until the *challah* sounds hollow when tapped on the bottom.

# Sabbath Quick Evening Meal Guide

AFTER READING THE book, this quick liturgy guide may be used for *Erev Shabbat.*

## Candle Lighting (*Hadlakat Nerot*)

Traditional Prayer

> *Baruch Atah Adonai, Eloheinu, Melech haolam asher kidishanu b'mitz'votav v'tzivanu l'had'lik ner shel Shabbat.*

> *Blessed are you, O Lord our God, Ruler of the universe, who has sanctified us by Your commandments and has commanded us to kindle the Sabbath lights.*

## Messianic Prayer

> *Baruch Atah Adonai, Eloheinu, Melech haolam asher kidishanu b'dam Yeshua v'tzivanu l'hiot or l'goyim.*

> *Blessed are you, O Lord our God, Ruler of the universe, who has sanctified us by the blood of Yeshua and inspired us to be a light to the nations.*

## Hand Washing (*Netilat Yadayim*)

Traditional and Messianic Prayer

> *Baruch Atah Adonai Eloheinu, Melech haolam asher kidishanu b'mitz'votav bietzeevanu al netilat yadayim.*

> *Blessed are you, O Lord our God, Ruler of the universe, who has sanctified us by your commandments and inspired us to wash hands.*

## Recited in Unison (Messianic response)

> *I dedicate my hands to Yeshua, the Messiah, to serve Him only.*

## Blessing the Children (*Birkat HaYeladim*)

For Girls

> *Y'simeikh Elohim k'Sara, Rivka, Rachel, Leah, Miriam, v' Elisheva.*

> *May God make you like Sarah, Rebekah, Rachel, Leah, Mary, and Elizabeth.*

For Boys

> *Y'simeikh Elohim k'Ephraim, Menashe, Yochanan, Mattai, v' Stefen.*

> *May God make you like Ephraim, Manasseh, John, Matthew, and Stephen.*

# Blessing Over the Wife (*Birkat HaEeshah*)

The father and the children stand in honor while the mother remains seated. They recite from the book of Proverbs.

*An accomplished woman who can find?*
*Her value is far beyond rubies.*
*Her husband's heart trusts in her,*
*and he lacks nothing valuable.*
*She brings him good and not harm*
*all the days of her life.*
*She selects wool and flax*
*and her hands work willingly.*
*She is like merchant ships,*
*bringing her sustenance from afar.*
*She rises while it is still night*
*and provides food for her household*
*and portions for her servant girls.*
*She considers a field and buys it.*
*From the fruit of her hands she plants a vineyard.*
*She girds herself with strength*
*and invigorates her arms.*
*She discerns that her business is good.*
*Her lamp never goes out at night.*
*She extends her hands to the spindle*
*and her palm grasps the spinning wheel.*
*She spreads out her palms to the poor,*
*and extends her hands to the needy.*
*She is not afraid of snow for her house,*
*for her whole household is clothed in scarlet wool.*
*She makes her own luxurious coverings.*
*Her clothing is fine linen and purple.*

*Her husband is respected at the city gates,*

*when he sits among the elders of the land.*

*She makes linen garments and sells them*

*and supplies sashes to the merchants.*

*Strength and dignity are her clothing,*

*and she laughs at the days to come.*

*She opens her mouth with wisdom—*

*a lesson of kindness is on her tongue.*

*She watches over the affairs of her household,*

*and does not eat the bread of idleness.*

*Her children arise and bless her,*

*her husband also praises her:*

*"Many daughters have excelled,*

*but you surpass them all."*

*Charm is deceitful and beauty is vain,*

*but a woman who fears* ADONAI *will be praised.*

*Give her the fruit of her hands.*

*Let her deeds be her praise at the gates (Proverbs 31:10–31 TLV).*

# Blessing over the Wine (Kiddush)

*"I am the vine, you are the branches. He who abides in Me, and I in Him, bears much fruit" (John 15:5 NKJV).*

## Traditional and Messianic Prayer

*Baruch Atah Adonai Eloheinu Melech haolam boray pre hagafen. Amen.*

*Blessed are You, O Lord our God, Ruler of the universe who creates the fruit of the vine. Amen.*

## Blessing over the Bread *(HaMotzi Lechem)*

### Traditional and Messianic Prayer

*Baruch Atah Adonai Eloheinu, Melech haolam hamotzi lechem min haaretz. Amen.*

*Blessed are You, O Lord our God, Ruler of the universe, who gives us bread from the earth. Amen.*

# Other References

BOTH JEWS AND Christians have taken Sabbath practice seriously throughout the centuries. There are many interesting facets to this historical issue. The following references may be useful for further study:

- http://www.friendsofsabbath.org/Further_Research /History%20of%20the%20Sabbatarian%20Movement /Sabbath_Observance_Through_The_Centuries.pdf
- http://www.sabbathtruth.com/sabbath-history/sabbath -through-the-centuries
- http://jerusalemcouncil.org/articles/reference/history -torah-observant-believers/

Then ADONAI spoke to Moses saying: "Speak to Benei-Yisrael, and tell them: These are the appointed moadim of ADONAI, which you are to proclaim to be holy convocations—My moadim. "Work may be done for six days, but the seventh day is a *Shabbat* of solemn rest, a holy convocation. You are to do no work—its is a *Shabbat* to ADONAI in all your dwellings"

—Leviticus 23:1–3 TLV